PRIZEWINNING ANIMALS

PRIZEWINNING PIGS

NANCY GREENWOOD

PowerKiDS press
NEW YORK

Published in 2023 by The Rosen Publishing Group, Inc.
29 East 21st Street, New York, NY 10010

First Edition

Portions of this work were originally authored by Jennifer Wendt and published as *Showing Pigs at the Fair*. All new material in this edition authored by Nancy Greenwood.

Editor: Kate Mikoley
Book Design: Andrea Davison-Bartolotta

Photo Credits: Cover inna Sochinska/Shutterstock.com; series art (animal outlines) Picture Window/Shutterstock.com; series art (gold ticket) Mar1kOFF/Shutterstock.com; series art (red ribbon) FMStox/Shutterstock.com; series art (pennant banner, gold ribbon) Tiax/Shutterstock.com; p. 4 Igor Stramyk/Shutterstock.com; p. 5 galitsin/Shutterstock.com; p. 6 acceptphoto/Shutterstock.com; p. 7 Fisenko Evgeny/Shutterstock.com; p. 9 Baloncici/Shutterstock.com; p. 11 Paulpixs/Shutterstock.com; p. 13 Elena Sherengovskaya/Shutterstock.com; p. 15 Zvigo17/Shutterstock.com; p. 17 yhelfman/Shutterstock.com; p. 19 CREATISTA/Shutterstock.com; p. 21 JNix/Shutterstock.com.

Library of Congress Cataloging-in-Publication Data

Names: Greenwood, Nancy, author.
Title: Prizewinning pigs / Nancy Greenwood.
Description: New York : PowerKids Press, [2023] | Series: Prizewinning animals | Includes index.
Identifiers: LCCN 2021042225 | ISBN 9781538386347 (set) | ISBN 9781538386354 (library binding) | ISBN 9781538386330 (paperback) | ISBN 9781538386361 (ebook)
Subjects: LCSH: Swine–Showing–Juvenile literature.
Classification: LCC SF394 .G74 2023 | DDC 636.4–dc23
LC record available at https://lccn.loc.gov/2021042225

Manufactured in the United States of America

Some of the images in this book illustrate individuals who are models. The depictions do not imply actual situations or events.

CPSIA Compliance Information: Batch #CSPK23. For Further Information contact Rosen Publishing, New York, New York at 1-800-237-9932.

CONTENTS

Let's Go TO THE FAIR!

The fair is a fun place to go on rides, play games, and see animals. You can show your own animals at the fair too. Do you have a pig? If so, you might want to show them at the fair.

Training a show pig takes time and hard work, but it can also be lots of fun. Showing your pig can help you learn even more about how to feed, **groom**, and care for them.

Training your pig can help you bond with your animal.

Pick a PRIZEWINNING PIG

There are many breeds, or kinds, of pigs. Choosing the right one can help you win at the fair. **Genetics** play a part in how your pig shows in the ring. Pick a pig that has a healthy history.

Once you have your pig, ask your **veterinarian** about a health plan. Read your fair guide to find out what **vaccinations** your pig needs. Pigs can get **diseases** easily. It's your job to keep your pig healthy.

ROAD TO WINNING

Going to see a show is a good way to learn which pigs do well in **competitions**. If you can, ask the winner about their pig's breed.

When looking for a pig, ask your **breeder** about the health of the animals' parents and siblings.

Time TO EAT!

Depending on the competition you enter, your pig may need to meet a certain weight **requirement**. Your veterinarian can help you figure out how much you need to feed your pig so it weighs what it needs to at the fair.

A veterinarian can also tell you what kinds of foods your pig needs. Whether your animal needs to make weight or not, feeding them the right variety of foods will keep them healthy. Foods pigs eat include grains, pig pellets, and vegetables.

ROAD TO WINNING

Always make sure your pig has lots of clean, fresh water to drink.

For baby pigs, the best food is their mother's milk. If that's not available, baby pigs can be fed special food from a bottle.

Lead THE WAY

Just like you, your pig needs daily exercise in order to stay healthy and strong. One way you should exercise your show pig is to take them for walks.

Start walking with your pig when it's young so it gets used to being led. Use a livestock cane to guide your pig and show them where to go. You will also use a livestock cane or pole to guide your pig in the show ring.

Pigs can be **stubborn**, so don't worry if it takes time for your pig to follow your lead.

Keeping it CLEAN

Pigs are known for being dirty animals that enjoy a good roll in the mud. Your show pig, however, will need to be clean and groomed on show day.

A few months before the fair, start getting your pig used to baths. Pigs like the water, so it should be fun! Use a gentle soap and make sure to scrub your pig's feet and clean its ears. Be careful not to get water inside your pig's ears though.

ROAD TO WINNING

You should brush your pig every day. This will make its hair fuller and help its skin stay healthy.

Small pigs can be washed in a tub. For larger pigs, you may want to use a hose.

Ready TO GO

Don't be afraid to ask for help getting ready for the fair. Ask a friend or family member to pretend to be a judge so you can practice for the show. Keep your pig between you and the judge and walk back and forth. Never put your cane between the pig and the judge.

Make sure to have your **registration papers**, cane, and supplies all in one place. This way, you won't forget anything when it's time to go to the fair.

ROAD TO WINNING

Remember to pack all the supplies you might need. This includes a brush, a spray bottle, a cloth, a livestock cane, treats, an extra bucket, ropes, and your show clothes.

Don't forget to take plenty of food for your pig to the fair. Bring your own feed pan and a separate pan for your pig's water too.

Show DAY

The first thing you should do when you get to the fair is check in. Then, find your pen and give your pig fresh bedding, water, and food. You won't be with your pig the whole time, so you want to make sure they're comfortable while you're gone.

Throughout the day, check on your pig and clean up any messes. The more comfortable and calm your pig is before the show, the more likely they are to do well in the ring.

There might be a lot of time before it's your pig's turn in the ring. Fresh bedding can help them stay comfortable and relax.

Hitting THE RING

Make sure your pig is clean before show time. Brush your pig, and make sure their ears, eyes, and **snout** are clean and shiny. You can give them a quick bath at the fair, but be sure to leave plenty of time for them to dry before entering the ring.

When it's your turn, remember to smile, and be respectful of the judges. Stay calm and **confident**. You worked hard to get here. Make sure to have fun!

ROAD TO WINNING

The judge will want to see your pig from all sides. Be sure to show the front, back, and sides. Thank the judge when your turn is over.

Your pig isn't the only one who needs to be well groomed for the show. Make sure your clothes are clean and your hair is brushed too!

Goodbye FOR NOW!

If you and your pig did really well, you might win a ribbon. But winning isn't the best thing about showing pigs. Making new friends, learning about your animal, and practicing fair-showing skills are just some of the things you were able to do because of the show!

Don't forget to thank everyone who helped you get ready for the fair. Clean up your pig's area and gather your supplies. Then, it's time to say goodbye to your new friends and head home!

If you can, ask the judges what you did well and what you could do better. This will help you do better in your next show!

GLOSSARY

breeder: Someone who keeps and cares for animals in order to produce more animals of a certain kind.

competition: An event in which people try to win.

confident: Having a feeling or belief that you can do something well.

disease: Illness.

genetic: Relating to genes, or tiny parts of a cell passed along from parent to offspring that decide specific features in the offspring, such as eye color.

groom: To clean.

registration papers: An official record of information.

requirement: Something that is needed or that must be done.

snout: An animal's nose and mouth.

stubborn: Not wanting to change one's ways.

vaccination: A shot that keeps a person or animal from getting a certain sickness.

veterinarian: A doctor who is trained to treat animals.

FOR MORE INFORMATION

BOOKS

Arnold, Quinn M. *Pigs*. Mankato, MN: Creative Education, 2020.

London, Martha. *Baby Pigs*. Minneapolis, MN: Cody Koala, 2021.

Wilson, Paula M. *Mini Pigs*. North Mankato, MN: Capstone Press, 2019.

WEBSITES

FFA
www.ffa.org
Future Farmers of America is an education-based organization for students interested in farming.

4-H
4-h.org
Through 4-H programs, children can learn new skills and take part in hands-on projects.

Pig
kids.nationalgeographic.com/animals/mammals/facts/pig
Learn more about pigs on this website.

Publisher's note to educators and parents: Our editors have carefully reviewed these websites to ensure that they are suitable for students. Many websites change frequently, however, and we cannot guarantee that a site's future contents will continue to meet our high standards of quality and educational value. Be advised that students should be closely supervised whenever they access the internet.

INDEX